Becoming
—a—
Magistrate

Becoming
a
Magistrate

Megan Harrison, JP

KOGAN
PAGE

First published in 1994

Apart from any fair dealing for the purposes of research or
private study, or criticism or review, as permitted under the
Copyright, Design and Patents Act , 1988, this publication
may only be reproduced, stored or transmitted, in any form
or by any means with the prior permission in writing of the
publishers, or in the case of reprographic reproduction in
accordance with the terms of licences issued by the
Copyright Licensing Agency. Enquiries concerning
reproduction outside those terms should be sent to the
publishers at the undermentioned address:

Kogan Page Limited
120 Pentonville Road
London N1 9JN

© Megan Harrison 1994

British Library Cataloguing in Publication Data

A CIP record for this book is available from the British
Library.

ISBN 0-7494-1245-3

Typeset by Books Unlimited (Nottm), Rainworth, NG21 0JE
Printed and bound in Great Britain by
Biddles Ltd, Guildford and King's Lynn

Contents

Acknowledgements

I would like to thank the many people who have helped in the preparation of this book, particularly Mike Watkins of the Leamington Spa Magistrates' Courts and Rosemary Thomson, OBE JP of the Magistrates' Association.

Note: Though all case studies in this book are real, names and some other details have been changed.

Masculine pronouns are used mainly in this book to avoid awkward grammatical constructions. In most instances, feminine pronouns can be used interchangeably.

1. What is a magistrate?

A magistrate is an ordinary man or woman who, for no payment, plays a vital rôle in the administration of the system of justice in England and Wales. There is a different arrangement in Scotland, but members of the local community still have an important part to play.

Magistrates' courts are responsible for hearing a wide variety of cases, totalling more than 96 per cent of all criminal cases coming before the courts. Many of the people who appear before the court are drivers charged with motoring offences, though offending motorists often either pay a fixed penalty or deal with the matter by post. Other very common offences include burglary, violence, drunkenness, theft, failing to pay fines and family maintenance agreements, criminal damage, and having no television licence. Magistrates also decide whether or not to grant bail for cases which are not completed that day, commit serious cases to Crown Court for trial, and hear matters such as those brought by trading standards or environmental health officers and the Department of Social Security.

Family panels help broken families to make decisions for the future of their children. Where the parents can agree who should care for the children day by day, and when the other parent will be able to see them, the magistrates may just confirm these arrangements. But when the parents cannot agree, the magistrates will have to make decisions for the welfare of the children. Family panels also make orders for care proceedings when children are abused, make maintenance orders and deal with the adoption of children.

Magistrates also decide whether an individual or premises should hold a licence to sell alcohol or a gaming licence, enforce previous non-payment of fines or civil debts, and hear cases involving youths.

In England and Wales, magistrates are chosen because they are personally suitable and of good repute, and also so that the mix of people on the bench broadly reflects the mix of people in the community which it serves. Although they do not hear cases where they know any of the people involved, local knowledge can be useful. It is helpful to be able to name the local accident black spot and then describe the particular traffic conditions. It is also easier for licensing magistrates to learn the local reputations of the various pubs, clubs and bingo halls when they live nearby.

Magistrates are appointed to the office of Justice of the Peace, and are entitled to use the letters 'JP' after their names. They sit in magistrates' courts and are often referred to as either 'magistrates' or 'justices'. For most practical purposes, there is no difference between the terms, and they are often used interchangeably, as they will be in this book. Strictly speaking, there is a difference. The term 'magistrate' is also used for stipendiary magistrates, who are legally qualified, paid magistrates who sit alone. Most stipendiary magistrates sit in London, though some other large cities are also now employing them. If a clerk to the justices expects a particular case to be lengthy, he may ask a stipendiary magistrate to sit temporarily at the court in question.

Most law-abiding people have never been inside a magistrates' court. Even many of those convicted of motoring offences deal with the whole matter by post, without a thought for the processes involved. Criminals, on the other hand, do appear in a magistrates' court. Those accused of the most minor offences ranging up to those ultimately convicted of the most infamous of murders will all appear before magistrates. In total, more than 99 per cent of all criminal cases are heard by magistrates at some point.

In addition to hearing criminal cases in both the adult and youth courts, magistrates grant (or refuse!) applications for betting, gaming and alcohol licences; make arrangements for the family when a marriage breaks down; arrange for children who are to be taken into care or adopted; sign search warrants and warrants for the arrest of people; endorse passport photographs; sit on various administrative committees and panels as well as many other tasks.

But who undertakes all this work? Around 30,000 lay magistrates, usually sitting three at a time, each give an average of 35 sessions lasting 4 hours every year. That adds up to a staggering 4 million man-hours a year. Is it any wonder that successive governments, reviews and commissions have all recommended the continuing need for a lay magistracy? Even if a paid staff was allowed to sit alone, at an average 39-hour working week, 48-week year, more than 700 people would have to be employed to complete the same volume of work.

So it is obviously important from a cost and logistic point of view that magistrates continue to adjudicate in both criminal and civil matters. Are there any other benefits to having teams of people with no formal legal training or knowledge decide the guilt or innocence of the people who appear before them? Undoubtedly – yes.

Community service

Magistrates are chosen from a wide cross-section of the community in which they serve. As well as choosing people who are personally suitable, the selection panels have a duty to balance the bench as far as is possible in terms of sex, race, education, income, political views and the places in which the magistrates live. The members of a particular bench should reflect the community which it serves. In addition, all magistrates should live or work in the area covered by the court (called a petty sessional division), or within 15 miles of its boundaries. This is so that they will have a good knowledge of any local problem areas. Since most magistrates sit only once every week or two, the rest of their lives are lived with the same mixture of interests, worries and family circumstances as the people who appear before them. Although magistrates do not hear cases where they know any of the people involved, including witnesses and solicitors, a neighbour may appear before colleagues. In these cases, magistrates must not discuss the neighbour or the circumstances with colleagues.

This living in the community and part-time service prevents magistrates from becoming too far removed from ordinary people. Magistrates *are* ordinary people. They do not all belong to the same golf club, or commute on the same trains. They do not even sit with the same colleagues each time, but they do have a wide understanding of human nature. This ability to remain down to earth and of the people is a great advantage to many of the defendants who appear before the court. It keeps the magistrates closer to the communities they serve than the sometimes rarefied atmosphere which can occur among members of a profession with a common jargon and common problems.

Many of the people who appear before the courts are unemployed or earn only small wages. A panel of magistrates who reflect their community is likely to have a greater understanding of the problems of trying to bring up a family with little money than highly paid judges, solicitors and barristers. That said, even when they appreciate the problems which may lead to some types of crime, magistrates do not condone this behaviour. It is, however, easier for them to make the necessary punishment fit the criminal as well as the crime.

Do people feel that justice, as dispensed by people with no formal legal training, is fair and just? On the whole, they do. Modern magistrates undertake extensive training, both before they first sit and regularly afterwards. They are kept up to date with changes in the law, as it affects them, and take specific courses before starting to work in the youth or family courts or on the licensing and betting panels.

It is common sense that whatever the defendant is accused of is against the law. A large majority of defendants plead guilty. The permitted sentences for the various offences are laid down, within a range showing the maximum and minimum allowed. So the two problems confronting magistrates are deciding whether or not a defendant pleading not guilty actually committed the crime or not, and if so, where along the scale the sentence should fall. An in-depth knowledge of the relevant laws is not needed, and magistrates have training to help them weigh the prosecution and defence evidence and give a reasoned decision. If all else fails, and someone feels wrongly convicted or harshly sentenced, an appeal can be made to the Crown Court.

Modern courts are very streamlined. Although the major crimes which hit the headlines are tried in the crown courts, magistrates deal with around 97 per cent of all criminal cases. They also examine the evidence in the other 3 per cent of cases, and commit the defendant for trial at the Crown Court if there is sufficient evidence to show that there is a case to answer – known as a *prima facie* (at first sight) case to answer. In these cases, the magistrates do not try the case, or weigh the relative merits of the evidence presented. They simply carry out a preliminary check that the prosecution has evidence of the defendant's guilt that should be heard in the Crown Court.

Not everyone who appears before a magistrates' court is a criminal, however. Prospective licensees of pubs and off-licences have to come to court to apply formally for a licence to sell alcohol. Similarly, if a licensee wishes to open later for a wedding reception, party or other special occasion, an application has to be made in court. Schools, charities and clubs who want to sell beer and wine at a fund-raising event also have to apply for an occasional permission to sell liquor.

When a marriage breaks down, the family court has to ensure that the arrangements for the children are satisfactory. Again, magistrates undertake specific training before they sit at family courts. In many cases, the parents agree who will care for the children day by day, the times when the other parent will be able to see them and maintenance payments. If these proposals are satisfactory, the magistrates will confirm them. But sometimes parents cannot agree, and the magistrates have to decide what will be in the best interests of the children. In these cases, the parents will be told the arrangements for their children, and will have to comply.

Family courts also hear the evidence and decide whether children should be taken into care. The situations vary, but children can be taken into care if 'the court is satisfied that the child is suffering, or is likely to suffer, significant harm; and that the harm or likelihood of harm is attributable to the care given to the child, or likely to be given to the child if a care order is not made, not being what would be reasonable to expect a parent to give him; or the child being beyond parental care' (Children Act, 1989). Parents whose children are of school age and not receiving full-time education can also be prosecuted in the Criminal Court, and the children can be taken into care as a last resort. Applications for adoption are considered.

It is an unpleasant fact that much crime in modern Britain is committed by people under 18 years old. All but the most serious of these cases are heard by magistrates, again after undertaking specific training. Youth courts are slightly different from normal adult courts – they are not open to the public, the press representatives are not allowed to publish the names of the defendants, and the proceedings are usually rather less formal. That said, most magistrates do their best to deter young criminals from a potential life of crime while trying to protect the rest of us from the actions of the young hooligans who sometimes appear before them. The parents of young offenders are encouraged, and generally expected, to attend the court, and to take greater responsibility for the actions of their children.

Other duties

More experienced magistrates are asked to take a share of the Saturday, bank holiday and crown court duties. Saturday and bank holiday sittings are sometimes needed because the police are allowed to hold suspects for a limited time only before either charging them with an offence or releasing them from custody. Someone arrested on the Friday evening of a bank holiday weekend cannot be held until Tuesday before being brought to court, so magistrates must be available to sit at these times. Newspapers sometimes carry banner headlines about battles between rival gangs, or football hooligans, who appear before magistrates on a bank holiday Monday. Where those involved plead guilty, the system offers a speedy and efficient way of punishing the behaviour and returning the offenders to their own homes.

Magistrates sit in the Crown Court to help the judge to hear appeals referred from magistrates' courts. If a defendant feels wrongly convicted, or rightly convicted but harshly sentenced, an appeal can be made to the Crown Court. Offenders with long records of previous convictions can be convicted in a magistrates' court and referred to the Crown Court for sentence. This happens when the magistrates do not feel that their sentencing powers are adequate to deal with a particular offender. Prospective licensees can also appeal if their application is turned down.

In all appeal cases, the judge usually has a magistrate from the same bench, though not one who was involved in the original case, and a magistrate from a neighbouring petty sessional division to decide if an error has been made. Since all magistrates are as human as anyone else, mistakes occasionally happen, and it is in the interest of justice that there is a way for them to be corrected. The judge and two magistrates are equal in authority when hearing an appeal.

The usual routes for appeals from one court to another are set out in the following chart:

House of Lords

Highest Court of Appeal
Only hears appeals on points of law
of major public importance

↑

<u>Court of Appeal</u>

↑   ↑

Civil Division   **Criminal Division**

Hears appeals in   Hears appeals in
civil cases   criminal cases

↑   ↑

<u>High Court</u>

Three divisions (Queen's Bench,   A Divisional Court of the
Family and Chancery) hear more   Queen's Bench hears appeals
complex, substantial and   →   on points of law from
important civil cases   magistrates' courts. There
              may be further appeal to the
              Criminal Division of the
              Court of Appeal

↑   ↑

County Court   **Crown Court**

Deals with most   Hears more serious
civil cases   criminal cases, cases
              committed for sentence
              by magistrates' courts
              and hears appeals from
              magistrates' courts

↑

Magistrates' Court

← Hears less serious criminal
cases, cases involving young
offenders, and some family
and civil cases

As well as the regular court appearances, magistrates sit on a wide variety of panels and committees. Some sit on panels called the Magistrates' Courts Committee, which is charged with establishing the overall administrative arrangements for courts in the area. Others attend Probation Liaison, area Probation Committee and Court Users' meetings to keep the bench represented and up to date with the activities of other agencies. Some magistrates sit on police authorities or on the Boards of Visitors of penal establishments. The licensing justices meet to discuss the local needs for pubs, off-licence shops, betting shops and bingo halls, to enable a reasoned policy to be implemented throughout the area. Some magistrates sit with non-magistrates on the Lord Chancellor's Advisory Committee, which interviews and appoints new magistrates to the bench. Others are elected to be the Bench Chairman, Deputy Chairman or to serve on a Chairmanship Committee. This selects magistrates with sufficient experience to attend chairmanship training to enable them to be court chairmen. Finally, all magistrates sitting on a particular bench are able to attend the bench meetings, often held quarterly, and discuss matters of interest to that particular bench.

2. Who can become a magistrate?

The short answer is – almost anyone. There are no essential prior qualifications, and very few restrictions. However, as each bench is expected to reflect all sections of the community it serves, not all suitable people are appointed. On the positive side, this means that applicants who are not typical magistrates may have an improved likelihood of being appointed. There are currently four women magistrates for every five men.

Some local political parties and charitable groups nominate suitable members for appointment, but these applicants have neither an advantage nor a disadvantage compared to those who put themselves forward for consideration. Potential magistrates must live or work in the area of the Commission of the Peace proposed.

Certain groups of people are not allowed to become magistrates, for different reasons:

1. Those with privileged information

- police officers
- members of the Special Constabulary
- civilian employees of the police force
- traffic wardens.

In order that justice is not only done, but seen to be done, it is important that magistrates are seen to be impartial. A policeman or civilian employee of the police force will necessarily hear rumours about local crimes and offenders around the police station. This information may make it difficult to come to court with an open mind.

2. Previous offenders
   - undischarged bankrupts
   - people who have been convicted of a serious offence
   - people who have been convicted of a number of minor offences, including those which carry fixed penalties.

People who have been convicted of offences themselves are likely to have an increased sympathy for the defendant, and may find it difficult to adjudicate fairly in other, similar, cases. Magistrates are also asked to resign if they are convicted of these offences, or are declared bankrupt, to ensure that the office of justice of the peace is not brought into disrepute. They are also asked to resign if convicted of drunken driving.

3. Conflicting interests
   - serving members of HM Forces
   - people whose work or community activities conflict with, or are not compatible with, the duties of a magistrate, such as solicitors and barristers working in the same courts, probation and prison officers who would have a wide knowledge of previous records and some youth and social workers, whose rôles might conflict

- people with a parent, child, brother or sister who is a police officer, traffic warden, magistrate or member of the special constabulary in the area covered by the court in which the magistrate would sit
- those with a close relative who works for the Crown Prosecution Service in the same area
- Members of Parliament, prospective candidates for election to Parliament and paid, full-time party political agents in the area of the court in question.

It is also possible that someone would not be appointed if their husband or wife fell into any of these categories.

Magistrates must be able and willing to do a fair share of the work of the bench, which implies good health and the available time. Some benches have separate morning and afternoon sessions, while others start in the morning and continue until the work is finished for the day. This means that instead of sitting one morning or afternoon each fortnight, a justice may only be called on once every three or four weeks – but may need to stay later in the day. Some petty sessional divisions ask magistrates to attend regularly on the same day every fortnight, while others have a moving rota to try to ensure that justices do not always sit with the same few colleagues. There is a certain amount of freedom to choose the system which best suits the justices serving a particular area, with guidance from the Clerk to the Justices.

Attendances

The Lord Chancellor defines an attendance as a morning or an afternoon sitting on the bench, and expects about 35, with not less than 26, attendances from each justice each year. As will always happen, some justices will find it easy to meet these conditions, and may sit considerably more times than the required minimum, while others will only manage the number set down. As well as looking into the reasons for a shortfall, the Lord Chancellor will also question the reason if a justice seems to be bearing an unduly high load. That said, situations can vary from year to year, and a temporary shortfall is likely to be viewed favourably.

All magistrates must be personally suitable in character, integrity and understanding, and new appointees must be aged 60 years or under. Many areas prefer to appoint new justices who are less than 55 years old, as there is a large amount of training in the early years. It is helpful to know that trained magistrates will be able to sit for some time before they are likely to retire owing to age or ill-health.

In most areas, the number of candidates exceeds the number of vacancies. The number of justices who serve in each area varies according to the amount of work needed, and no new justices will be appointed until someone retires or resigns, or until an increase in workload justifies further appointments. In order to maintain the balance of the bench, the appointment panel will try to ensure that representatives from all sections of the community are considered.

Once selected, new magistrates swear or affirm an oath of allegiance to Her Majesty the Queen, and also swear a judicial oath. Part of this oath involves swearing to uphold and administer the laws of the realm, and those with strong political or social convictions need to think carefully before they become a magistrate. The oath is to uphold *all* laws, not just those it is convenient to uphold. For example, many justices resigned when they found themselves having to convict and sentence people who failed to pay the Community Charge, which they felt was an unjust tax.

3. Selection of magistrates

How are magistrates chosen? The procedure is very lengthy and very rigorous. It is, after all, important to the defendants who appear before the courts that those chosen to hear their cases are the best possible people to decide the facts of the matter, adjudicate guilt or innocence, and pass sentence if necessary.

Each bench has its own needs, depending on the quantity and nature of the work which comes before it. It is known how many magistrates are needed to deal with that amount of work, and no new appointments will be made unless someone retires from the bench or a general increase in work makes extra appointments necessary. So no new magistrates at all may be appointed in some areas for a particular year. However, with a total of around 30,000 magistrates, it is likely that some will retire each year owing to ill health or on reaching 70 years of age.

Selection panels need to consider the total number of magistrates needed for the area in the coming year, the likely requirement for future years and the numbers likely to be retiring in the near future. They then agree the number of new appointments to be made. In some years, there may be none. In others, a relatively large number of new appointments may be made. This might be because of an increasing workload, or because it is known that several retirements will soon occur. Allowance also has to be made for the few justices who move out of the area, and who can no longer be called on to serve. From an individual point of view, it is possible to be re-assigned to the bench in the new area, but this is not of help to the town which has been left short of magistrates.

Once a decision has been made about the number of new magistrates to be appointed, the panel will consider the current members of the bench, and compare these people with the local community. The aim is for every bench to reflect the community it serves in terms of social and economic factors. Each bench should also be balanced in itself. To achieve this, no more than 15 per cent of the members may have a similar job, several people who live in the same road will not be appointed, and a close relation of someone already on the bench is not allowed to be appointed. Too many university graduates would lead to an imbalance – but so too would the appointment of too many people with no academic qualifications at all.

Once the broad outline of the numbers and types of people who need to be appointed has been drawn up, the selection panel will consider the question of applicants. Political parties, charities and community groups are sometimes asked to suggest suitable people, although these nominees will have neither an advantage nor a disadvantage when it comes to being selected. Some people decide for themselves that they would like to perform this public service, while friends and employers sometimes suggest it. Selection panels and the Lord Chancellor's office also sometimes advertise in local and national newspapers for candidates.

All appointments to the office of justice of the peace are made by the Lord Chancellor, except for Lancashire, Merseyside and Greater Manchester, where they are made by the Chancellor of the Duchy of Lancaster using the same principles.

To ensure that the Lord Chancellor's staff have the best possible information about the potential justices in a petty sessional division, Lord Chancellor's Advisory Committees are appointed. Some are for a particular petty sessional division, while others recommend the appointments for several divisions. Since some large cities have several petty sessional divisions within their boroughs, while more rural divisions may cover several smaller towns, it is not possible to be precise about the coverage of each division.

The Lord Chancellor's Advisory Committees are made up of people of widely differing experience, drawn from the local community. Some are magistrates themselves, while others have different backgrounds. Prominent members of the local council or voluntary bodies are sometimes asked to sit. The Clerk to the Justices often acts as an observer.

Application

A person who wishes to become a magistrate must first fill in a lengthy application form, which is available from any magistrates' court. After the obvious questions of name, address, date and place of birth and nationality, the form asks about the family and health of the applicant. It goes on to enquire about educational qualifications, professional or trade qualifications and current and previous work, in much the same way as the application for a job. Questions are asked about other voluntary and community work, and any other experience which may be relevant to the work of a justice of the peace. To ensure that all magistrates are personally suitable, questions need to be answered about any criminal convictions or court orders, including maintenance orders. These do not automatically disqualify a candidate from appointment, but must be disclosed. The Rehabilitation of Offenders Act does not apply, and the information may be checked.

The final questions ask whether the applicant has been a justice of the peace anywhere else, or has been considered anywhere else, and invites the candidate to state the reasons for wishing to become a magistrate.

The names and addresses of two sponsors, who should have known the candidate for at least two years, are required. These sponsors should read the completed application form, and sign in the appropriate place to signify their consent to sponsoring the applicant.

Once completed, the form should be returned to the Clerk to the Magistrates of the petty sessional division to which appointment is sought. This address is usually on the front of the form. Most courts acknowledge receipt of the completed form quite quickly. Unless the application has to be rejected quickly for an obvious reason, the sponsors will also be asked fairly soon to provide the necessary reference.

Although application forms can be completed and returned at any time of the year, once received, they have to abide by a strict timetable. All appointments (apart from those in Greater Manchester, Lancashire and Merseyside) have to be approved by the Lord Chancellor. To ensure that the Department has a reasonable throughput of work, each county has to submit its recommendations in a particular month, laid down by the Lord Chancellor's

Department. The selection panels have to work backwards from that month, allowing time for each stage, to arrive at the best time to hold meetings and interviews.

A particular petty sessional division might decide the number of new magistrates needed at the bench annual general meeting, usually held in October. A meeting of the Advisory Committee might be held in November or December, to decide from the applications received the most suitable candidates for interview. So someone who returned the forms in February or March might not hear anything at all for almost a year. If, in a particular year, it is decided that no new appointments need be made, it can be much longer between making the application and being invited to attend for interview.

Interview

Different panels have different ways of deciding which of several equally suitable candidates to appoint. Some just ask the candidates to attend for a formal interview, while others send one or two representatives to visit the potential justices in the more relaxed atmosphere of their own homes. This visit would be followed by a formal interview.

The interview can be a very daunting experience. There may be as many as a dozen people around a large desk, any of whom may ask questions. Depending on the applicant, these can vary from an employer's likely cooperation in giving the required leaves of absence, arrangements for childcare, empathy with people from varied backgrounds, or the level of support which can be expected from a husband or wife.

Although some of these questions may seem irrelevant or intrusive, it is important that new magistrates are able to commit themselves to the time needed to carry out the duties of a justice. If a spouse or employer is likely to prove unhelpful or awkward, the candidate needs to think carefully before proceeding further. That said, employers are encouraged to give staff who are magistrates paid time off for judicial duties, and they may be obliged to allow magistrates unpaid leave even if they are reluctant. However, some justices have found that, given the choice between promoting a magistrate and a colleague who is not a justice, some employers prefer the person who does not need to take leaves of absence from work. Other companies actively promote community service by staff members.

Many selection panels will give the candidates a case study, and ask how the defendant would be treated if brought before the court. There will probably be a little time allowed to consider the response to these studies. These are often difficult cases, with awkward social implications, and have no particular right or wrong answer. They serve to examine the candidate's ability to form a reasoned judicial decision. In most cases, the interview panel is more interested in the reasons the candidate gives for the decision, rather than what the decision actually is.

It is likely that the potential magistrate will be asked why he wishes to become a justice of the peace. Again, there is no real right or wrong answer, but the panel will be interested in the thought processes behind the answer. In all the questions, there is an underlying need to ensure that the candidates who are appointed are personally suitable, and that as well as forming reasoned decisions on the bench, they will uphold the dignity of the court system and the magistracy. Magistrates who regularly pay speeding fines or parking tickets are not master criminals, but also do not regularly uphold the law of the land in which we all live. It does not reflect well when the newspapers report lurid details of the lives of those who pass judgement on others in any capacity.

At the end of the interview, the candidate will be thanked for attending, with no indication of the decision of the panel. This is because the panel will not make a selection until all candidates have been seen, so that the most suitable candidates who contribute best to the overall balance of the bench can be selected. It may be some time before the candidate hears whether or not an appointment has been made. It is, in fact, usually a case of 'no news is good news', as the unsuccessful candidates will be notified, while those who are recommended will hear nothing for quite some time.

Time commitment

As well as assessing the suitability of the candidates, the interview panel will usually give the prospective magistrates some idea of the commitment expected of them. Some explanation of the rota system which operates on a particular bench may be given. Some petty sessional divisions have court houses in two (or, occasionally, more) adjacent towns, and magistrates may be expected to sit at either, as the rota dictates. Some divisions ask justices to sit at a regular, predictable, time and place, such as alternate Thursday mornings. Others have a more random rota to enable magistrates to experience sitting with a greater variety of colleagues. Some rotas indicate one team of magistrates for the morning sessions and another team for afternoons, while others work on a daily rota, with justices staying until the work is completed. All the different systems aim to keep the work flowing smoothly through the courts, with all justices contributing about equally in terms of numbers of sittings. The convenience of witnesses and the court staff is also considered.

There are usually three courses of action open to the selection panel – to recommend appointment, to refuse appointment, or to recommend appointment in a later year.

If the candidate is refused appointment, a letter giving the decision may be received within a few weeks. If the candidate is held over for another year, a letter giving this response may be received quite quickly, or may take longer. Applications are sometimes held in this way when the panel decides that the candidate would personally make a good magistrate, but would not at present help to balance the bench. This could be because there are already several justices with a similar job, or other similar social circumstances. If a candidate is recommended for appointment, nothing will be heard.

The details of all applicants who are successful at this stage will be sent to the Advisory Committee. This Committee will consider the selections for several petty sessional divisions to ensure that the balance is maintained. This is because although justices usually serve a particular petty sessional division, they are generally appointed to the Commission of the Peace for the whole of the county, and may be asked to serve temporarily on another bench. Experienced magistrates also have some duties in the Crown Court, and again, the balance of the bench for the whole county is taken into account.

If the recommendation is approved by the County Advisory Committee, the candidate's name will be forwarded to the Lord Chancellor's Department (or the office of the Chancellor of the Duchy of Lancaster) for approval. If not, he will receive a letter telling him that his application has not been successful.

Appointment

A new magistrate may not be aware of the appointment until a letter addressed to 'Mrs M Harrison, JP' drops through the letter box. 'Funny, what's this?' may be the first thought, until the envelope is opened and the text of the letter of appointment read.

Shortly afterwards, a letter of congratulation from the Clerk to the Justices will usually be received. This will give details of preliminary arrangements for the swearing of the oaths and the induction training sessions.

Many benches will hold an informal meeting of all the newly appointed justices, perhaps with the chairman of the bench present to welcome his new colleagues. This meeting will enable the magistrates to begin to get to know each other, and discover the most convenient times and dates for the training sessions. The new magistrates will also be told how to enter the court through the official magistrates' entrance, and any car parking arrangements or other local administrative details. If it has not been done at the interview, the new justices may be offered a tour of the court building, and will be introduced to some of the court staff.

Oaths

The swearing of the oaths is a very formal and solemn occasion. A judge, dressed in full judicial robes and wig, hears the oaths in a formal ceremony. Each new justice of the peace in turn either takes the New Testament and swears, or solemnly affirms, his allegiance to Her Majesty the Queen, and his willingness to administer the laws of the realm. He then signs a copy of the text of the oaths, which is countersigned by the judge and filed. Guests of the new magistrates and some existing members of the bench often gather, with the judge and any other invited guests, for tea and biscuits to welcome the new colleagues to the bench.

Technically, the newly appointed justices hold office from the moment they swear the oaths. In practice, they do not begin to sit in court until they have completed the induction training, and observed in court on several occasions.

4. Training for magistrates

Although justices are called 'lay', in the sense that they are not qualified in law in the same way as solicitors and barristers, they do have to undertake training. If the training requirements are not met, a magistrate will be asked to resign from the bench.

In fact, magistrates do not need a detailed knowledge of the law. The magistrates' clerk who sits in every court is legally qualified, and advises on points of law as they arise. Magistrates do, however, need to be able to weigh the relative merits of often conflicting evidence to decide whether or not the defendant is guilty. If so, they need to weigh the seriousness of this offence in the light of any aggravating or mitigating circumstances to decide the appropriate sentence.

More experienced magistrates need to be trained in chairmanship skills, youth court procedures, family courts, licensing panels and gaming committees. In the past, experience and the recommendation of colleagues on the bench were enough for an individual to sit in these more specialised courts. Current thinking has ensured that magistrates are properly trained to make the important decisions which face them each time they sit.

Before they begin to sit, new magistrates are required to complete an induction training course. This continues during the first three years of service, and should be completed before the end of that time. Before the first sitting, new justices are expected to observe in court and receive a course of lectures from either the training officer or the clerk to the justices.

In either case, the person responsible will be an experienced magistrates' clerk, who is legally trained. He is also likely to have received training in how to deliver training courses! Most sessions are fairly informal, but will use a wide mixture of experience and case studies to provide the information needed to give the magistrates the confidence to sit in court.

Most of the magistrates will have observed in court before the start of the formal training course, so the training officer will be able to draw on those cases to illustrate the points being made. There is usually an emphasis on participation and open-ended questions designed to make the magistrates think for themselves, rather than formal lectures. That said, there is a large amount of information for the magistrates to assimilate.

The topics which must be covered before the magistrates can adjudicate include court formalities; human awareness, including awareness of the different ethnic, cultural and religious backgrounds of those with whom they have to deal as witnesses or defendants; how to assess the often conflicting evidence presented to the court; the importance of bail hearings, and whether to remand defendants on bail or in custody; decisions about mode of trial; the committal proceedings for those cases which are sent to the Crown Court; the usual course of a criminal trial; the reports available to the court; the sentences available to the court; motoring matters; the place of legal aid, and many other related matters.

Newly appointed magistrates will always sit with more experienced colleagues. Although they will have an equal voice with these colleagues, and will be equally responsible for the decisions made, colleagues and court clerks are usually only too pleased to explain their reasons for choosing a particular course of action. As well as helping the new magistrate to gain experience, it is also good for those who have been sitting for many years to examine their own decision-making procedures, to ensure that they do not become stale or cynical.

Continuing training

After the first three years, training continues. The minimum required by the Lord Chancellor's Department is currently 12 hours every 3 years – not a great commitment. Many of the same topics will again be covered, but with a different emphasis in the light of some experience. New legislation, and the ways in which it affects magistrates' courts, are discussed, together with other subjects of interest to the particular group.

In most cases, formal lectures are kept to a minimum, and the emphasis is on practical exercises to develop the skills required to be an effective magistrate. In later years, magistrates may choose to undertake training in chairmanship skills, family courts, youth courts, licensing panels, betting and gaming sessions and general topics of interest. Obviously, not all magistrates will sit in all types of court, even over many years. As in all occupations, there is room for choice and personal interests. Someone with no interest in children or teenagers is unlikely to want to sit in youth or family courts, while others may have no interest in liquor or betting licences.

Induction training

All the newly appointed magistrates will undertake their induction training together. Sometimes, the new magistrates from several petty sessional divisions will undertake their induction training together. This not only enables the clerk to instruct several groups simultaneously, but will also permit the larger group to gain the experience of all the court observations undertaken by the group. Senior magistrates are often involved in the training of new colleagues. The only disadvantage is that the group of new magistrates will get to know each other fairly well during this initial period of learning, but will not sit together for some time, as inexperienced magistrates always sit with more experienced colleagues.

Even with a small group, the court observations will be different, as different people will have different days and times available to them. These differing experiences of the courts will be of interest both to the rest of the group and to the clerk, who will usually be only too happy to use the queries inevitably raised to illustrate the points he is making.

More experienced magistrates are usually willing to help trainee colleagues on the bench by explaining what the background to a particular case is, and why a particular decision was arrived at.

Although British justice demands that most court cases are heard in public, the deliberations of the justices are confidential, and so are some of the reports available to them. For example, after a defendant has pleaded guilty or been proved guilty after a trial, his previous criminal record is made available to the magistrates in order to help them arrive at a suitable sentence. If the record is long or the justices are considering a custodial or community sentence, they will request a pre-sentence report, to be produced by the Probation Service, to help them to decide between the various sentencing options open to them. The preparation of these reports can take some time, so adjournments are common. These reports are not available to the general public, and hence not to the trainee magistrates, who might wonder why a particular sentence was imposed.

In many cases, there are guidelines produced by the Magistrates' Association available to the magistrates to help them to arrive at their decisions. During the induction training, the relative importance of different evidence will be discussed. This is important to both individual defendants and to the public perception of courts, as people often wonder why two cases with many apparent similarities have very differing outcomes. Even when two people are jointly charged with the same offence, different decisions may be made. If two young men are accused of assaulting a police officer after a Saturday evening in the pub, the one with no previous criminal record and a stable family background, with parents prepared to take responsibility for their son, may be granted unconditional bail until the date of the trial. In contrast, the one with no fixed address and a history of violence may only be granted bail on the condition that he lives at a bail hostel and does not enter licensed premises until the next hearing.

To someone who only reads a report of the committal for trial in the local newspaper, the fact that one is allowed to remain at home while the other has to live in a bail hostel might seem unfair. But the justices will have considered the evidence for each young man separately, and arrived at a fair decision for both.

To many people, a court room is a daunting place. Although no one wears a wig, and only the court usher wears a gown, the male solicitors and magistrates generally wear business suits and the women will usually dress in a similarly formal style. Anyone who speaks to the magistrates will stand, and the magistrates are addressed as 'Sir', 'Madam' or 'Your Worships'. This is not because there is anything special about the three particular people who are sitting that day – it is to maintain the dignity of the court, and it is the office of justice of the peace which is being addressed as 'Sir' or 'Madam', not the individual. But this formality can be an added strain to someone unfamiliar with it.

It is sad that the innocent people who have to go to court as witnesses often fear the ordeal more than the habitual criminals who appear regularly before the magistrates, and who may only be wondering what the sentence might be this time.

The vast majority of all trials and other hearings are held in open court, so that everything is open to inspection. To ensure total fairness, any magistrate who knows any of the people involved in a particular case will not sit at any hearing for that case. This can include matters against a company for which the magistrate works or holds shares, cases involving a neighbour or work colleague and those where a member of the family or a friend may be called as a witness.

All defendants are presumed innocent until the prosecution has produced enough evidence to prove guilt. It is only natural that if someone with 26 previous convictions for shoplifting is again before the court accused of shoplifting, observers may think guilt is obvious. So any magistrate with knowledge of the defendant's previous criminal record will not sit on a new case. This can cause problems, as habitual criminals with many convictions can eventually run out of magistrates who have not seen his record! In the interests of justice, the court clerk will sometimes ask magistrates from a neighbouring petty sessional division to hear a case.

Many magistrates get to the end of the evidence in a trial and feel that they still do not know what really happened. The prosecution tells one story, the defence tells another, and both produce witnesses to back up their version of events. The magistrates will be sure that the truth lies somewhere between the two extremes, but may have differing opinions about the exact point between. One example is the case of John and Paul, and the broken car window. The two youths were not friends, though they lived close to each other, and had vaguely known each other since their school days. They had several friends in common. Paul passed his driving test, and was given a car which had been owned by his father. He was driving proudly round the housing estate where he lived, when he saw a group of his friends. He naturally stopped to pass the time of the evening with his friends, and to let them admire his new car.

John and a small group of friends arrived, and, as they knew several members of the first group, stopped to join the conversation. The two stories agreed up to this point. But Paul then alleged that John and Lee climbed into the front passenger seat of his car, accidentally knocking the rear view mirror off its mounting. Paul asked them to get out of the car, and when they did not, pushed them out. John went round to the driver's door, opened it, and started kicking and punching Paul in the face. When Paul managed to close the door, John continued to kick, eventually damaging the door and breaking the window.

John's version of events was that he and Daniel (not Lee) had climbed into the car, the mirror had been dislodged, and that Paul had then become very violent. He had got out of the car, walked round to the passenger door, and dragged John and Daniel out of the car. He had then leaned John on the bonnet, and started to punch him. John admitted to trying to defend himself from the attack, and said that he had rolled off the bonnet, and walked round the car by the least congested route, which happened to be beside the driver's door. Paul had followed, and kicked out at John. When John evaded the kick, Paul had been unable to stop the action, and had broken his own car window. The only reason he was bringing the case at all was that the insurance did not cover his own damage, and he was trying to make John pay for the damage to the car.

The magistrates felt that the whole case was rather a mountain built from a molehill, and that neither young man had been particularly truthful. They could not even agree about the identity of the second youth who climbed into the car. Because John had pleaded not guilty, there was a short trial, which called as witnesses the police officers who had interviewed John and Paul. Interestingly, despite the two groups of friends, neither young man called any other witnesses. Both claimed that the matter was between the two of them, and did not want to get their friends involved.

After their deliberations, the magistrates did find John guilty, and sentenced him to pay compensation to the value of the damage, with community service. But the only undisputed facts were that Paul had a new car, the rear view mirror was knocked off during youthful horseplay, a fight took place, and the window was broken.

The skill of listening to two completely different versions of the same event and weighing the evidence appropriately, is one which comes with practice. In this case, three different magistrates might have found the matter not proved, and John not guilty of the damage.

Much time in court is taken up with bail decisions. All criminal cases enter the court system via the magistrates' courts. Magistrates are responsible for deciding whether or not to grant bail, and if so, with what conditions, for all these cases. At present (1994), except when the charge is rape or murder, there is a general presumption in favour of unconditional bail, though this is currently under review. The magistrates have to grant bail unless there is a valid reason not to do so. In the majority of cases, the defendant or his solicitor will ask for unconditional bail, and the prosecution will not offer any objections. Unconditional bail will be granted, which means that the defendant is free to leave the court. He may go about his daily life with no restrictions, but must attend court at the time and place stated, or will be in breach of bail, and a warrant may be issued for his arrest.

If the prosecution does object to unconditional bail, reasons must be given, and the magistrates will consider the case on its merits. If unconditional bail is not granted, the defendant will be given a bail record, completed by the clerk of the court using the decisions of the magistrates. This states the reasons for remanding in custody or for imposing conditions on the bail. Conditions can include a requirement to live at a stated address, a surety to be paid in the event of non-appearance at the next hearing, instructions not to associate with other named defendants to the same charges, to remain indoors between stated hours, to report to the police station at stated times, to stay out of licensed premises or not to interfere with witnesses. It is unlikely that all these conditions would be applied to any individual. Those that are imposed must be the result of valid grounds for restraint, as the presumption is that the liberty of innocent people is being restricted.

If unconditional bail is refused in the magistrates' court,

an application can be made to a high court judge or the Crown Court.

Since one of the reasons for refusing bail, or imposing conditions, is the defendant's previous record of failing to answer bail or committing further offences while on bail, the magistrates need to see the record of previous convictions. This naturally means that those justices will not be able to hear the case when it eventually comes to trial.

During their induction training, newly appointed magistrates are often divided into benches of three, and asked to consider their decision on a wide range of case studies. These are always a little artificial, because there is no real person present who can be questioned further. On the other hand, all the groups have exactly the same information, and identical guidelines. But even at this stage, it is uncommon for all the benches to give the same decision. One group of 24 new justices, asked to make a fictitious bail decision, came up with the whole range of options, from remand in custody to the sole condition of living at home and staying indoors from 7.00pm to 7.00am. Other benches imposed a wide range of conditions for the bail, including residence at a bail hostel, sureties to be paid in the event of non-appearance and reporting to the police station every evening.

Summary, indictable and either-way offences

Criminal offences in England and Wales are classified as summary offences, indictable offences or either-way offences. Summary offences are tried in a magistrates' court, after the issue of a summons. Indictable offences are tried on indictment in a crown court. Either-way offences, as the name implies, can be tried in either a magistrates' court or a crown court. In these cases, the defendant chooses whether the case should be heard by the magistrates or by a judge and jury. However, if the case seems particularly serious, the magistrates can decide that the case is not suitable for summary trial, and send the defendant to a crown court even if he would prefer to be tried by the magistrates. A case heard by the magistrates can also be sent to a crown court for sentencing, if the magistrates decide that the seriousness of the offence or the defendant's previous record indicate a sentence that is outside their powers.

In the vast majority of the hundreds of thousands of cases which are heard in magistrates' courts every year, the defendant pleads guilty to the offence with which he is charged. In these cases, the magistrates hear the facts of the matter from the prosecution, the guilty plea from the defendant and any plea of mitigation from the defence solicitor. In many motoring cases, the defendant does not even attend court. The magistrates have only to consider the offence together with the defendant's previous record, and decide the appropriate sentence.

A busy court complex with four separate courts working five days each week may only hear as few as six contested trials each month. This is partly because so many defendants plead guilty, and partly because many defendants in either-way cases elect to be tried by a judge and jury at the Crown Court. This leaves magistrates with relatively few long cases to hear. However, it is vitally important that the induction training includes a discussion about trial procedures.

It has been said that a British trial is a game with very elaborate rules. Though most defendants would disagree that the procedure is a game, there are indeed very formal rules laid down, in order to minimise the risk of an innocent person being convicted. In the event of uncertainty, the benefit of the doubt is always given to the defendant.

In addition, there is always the possibility of an appeal if the defendant (or his solicitor) is not satisfied with the result.

The induction training will demonstrate the course of a trial. Some groups may include rôle play activities, with different people playing the parts of the defendant, solicitor, prosecution, magistrates and witnesses. All newly appointed justices are encouraged to watch a trial in progress, to enable them to understand the processes involved.

In common with many other aspects of late twentieth-century life in Britain, magistrates' courts are inundated with paper. At the conclusion of a trial, or after a guilty plea, the magistrates will have many papers and documents to help them to arrive at a suitable sentence that fits both the crime and the criminal. If there is a previous criminal record, this will be taken into account. If the court wishes, the probation service can be asked to provide a pre-sentence report. This assesses the effect of the various sentences available to the court on both the defendant himself and on his family and, occasionally, any employer. When George was convicted of drink driving, he was sentenced to community service rather than imprisonment, partly because his employer stated that he was essential to the business, and that the jobs of 120 other people were dependent on George's contribution to the company.

The magistrates will also receive reports about the availability of support for sentences such as community service and violent offender groups.

Magistrates' courts have a wide range of sentencing powers, though there is always a maximum of 6 months in prison or a £5,000 fine for a single offence. If the previous record shows that a particular defendant should receive a higher sentence, he will be referred to the Crown Court for sentence.

The most common sentence in the magistrates' court is the fine. This is imposed for many offences, ranging from speeding, to assault, to theft. Other possible sentences include discharges, community service, probation and combination orders, driving licence endorsements and imprisonment. Inexperienced magistrates will quickly learn the maximum, minimum and usual sentences for a range of offences which are regularly heard. Sentence guidelines are available from the Magistrates' Association, which offer a starting point for consideration. Any aggravating or mitigating circumstances will enable the bench to make the sentence more or less than the guideline, to suit the person in question.

Motoring offences

A depressing number of the cases which appear in the courts are motoring offences. Contrary to press reports, these are not innocent motorists caught driving rather too fast. Most are far more serious cases of people driving while very drunk, often with no road tax, MOT or insurance. As well as the possibility of innocent pedestrians or drivers of other cars being seriously maimed or killed by these irresponsible drivers, these road users increase the cost of motoring for everyone. Again, the magistrates are given practice in balancing the different evidence to decide whether or not the offence has been committed, and if so, what the appropriate sentence is.

After the initial training course, magistrates will start to sit in court, hearing all types of cases. They will have an equal voice in the decisions of the bench, and be equally responsible for those decisions. Later in the first three years, there will be follow-up training sessions, which may include visits to local prisons and remand centres. These will enable the magistrates to fully understand the implications of the sentences they are required to pass.

Further training

Although the training commitment reduces after the initial period, there is still a need for further training. This might include more discussions about the topics covered in the induction training, but drawing on the early experience gained in court. This will enable the justices to continually examine their reasoning processes, and make sure that all decisions are fair and just. More experienced magistrates will receive training for crown court service, updates when laws or sentencing procedures are altered by Parliament, and the many other changes which can be made. Sometimes offences are moved from indictment only to being triable either way. Other offences are made summary-only offences. There is a constantly changing workload through the courts, and all magistrates need to be familiar with current practices.

Other magistrates may wish to serve on the specialist panels and committees, such as youth or family courts, betting, gaming or liquor licensing committees, or fine enforcement panels. Again, training both before starting these specialised areas and to keep up to date during service is often available.

After about five years' service, justices are often invited to chair some court sessions, and again, different skills are needed. The court chairman is responsible for maintaining the flow of work through the courts, as well as for stating the decisions and sentences of the bench. The chairman is responsible for ensuring that the discussion is properly structured, and covers all the relevant issues. He does not have any extra powers in the retiring room, and may be overruled by his colleagues on the day. Nevertheless, he will state the decision of the bench, and should not do as one chairman did when he announced 'My colleagues find you guilty, and sentence you to...'.

This ongoing training is the responsibility of the local training officer, who is often the clerk to the justices. He may provide the training himself, may join with colleagues from nearby petty sessional divisions to provide training for a wider group, or may book places for magistrates on suitable courses run by a local university or other institution. Some courses may be only one day, while others may offer a choice of a series of dates or a weekend course. Wherever possible, the training will be made to fit the constraints of the justices' jobs and family circumstances.

Many employers are happy to consider magistrate training as a benefit to their own companies – a magistrate who has taken a course in chairmanship skills, for example, might become more effective in meetings at work. Another justice who has completed a course in assessing evidence might be able to use this additional skill in his work.

5. The work of a magistrate

During the course of each working day, the court staff will prepare lists of the cases due to be heard in each court the next day. Some of these will have been planned for some time, but others will be new. The lists may run to many pages, with more than 30 cases to be heard in some courts. However, some will only occupy a few minutes. With experience, the listing clerk learns to estimate quite accurately the amount of work which can be sensibly handled in a day. On the other hand, some days have very little business, and the magistrates are free to leave by late morning.

Before they begin to hear the listed matters, the magistrates will hear the cases of the people who have been arrested by the police during the previous evening, and held in the police cells until brought before the court.

British justice does not allow anyone to be held for longer than is absolutely necessary without being heard. For example, Tina Smith was charged with criminal damage. The prosecution alleged that she had been arrested while fighting with a shopping centre security guard, after kicking a hole in the glass door of the centre. She also said that she had torn some tiles from the bus station roof, but the police were still investigating this. Tina had a long record of previous convictions for criminal damage, including several committed while on bail. By a coincidence, the duty solicitor that day had represented Tina in the past, and was willing to accept her instructions on this occasion.

After consultation, Tina listened while the court clerk read the charges to her, and consented to a summary trial. She made a plea of not guilty, and asked for bail. Because of her previous record of committing further offences while on bail, Tina was remanded in custody until the trial date, some three weeks later.

Duty solicitor

Many courts operate a duty solicitor scheme. Local solicitors with experience in criminal cases take it in turns to spend time in the court, waiting for people who have no solicitor to appear. This is so that all defendants can have an equal right to representation. Some people do not realise that they can have a solicitor, some think that they cannot afford one because they do not know of the legal aid scheme, and others choose to remain unrepresented. Those who have received no legal advice at all can consult the duty solicitor. He cannot give advice under this scheme anywhere except in the court house, and his advice may well be to brief a solicitor as quickly as possible. In this way, he may sometimes gain new clients – a fair exchange for the work done without pay.

In some cases, acting as duty solicitor, he will tell the court that he has no previous knowledge of the case, but that the defendant has indicated that he consents to summary trial, and pleads guilty. The court clerk or solicitor will then explain any sentence or bail conditions to the defendant. Although the duty solicitor will do his best for the defendant at the time of the hearing, he will not follow the case any further, or do any other work for that person, unless specifically instructed to do so. The court clerk can also advise unrepresented defendants, but not in the presence of the magistrates.

During the course of the day, the magistrates deal with a range of cases where the defendant does not appear. Sometimes, these may be dealt with before the start of the other business or at the end of the session. Others are used to occupy the time between the end of one case and the start of the next, while the solicitors and witnesses are being called into the court.

One such case was that of Stephen Fain who was accused of driving at 51 mph in a 30 mph area. The court clerk read a letter from his solicitor, pleading guilty and apologising to the court for the delay in producing the necessary documents. In motoring matters, the driver of the car or other vehicle usually has to produce documents to prove that it was taxed, had a valid MOT certificate, and was insured for that driver at the time of the offence. The driver will also have to produce his own licence to drive that type of vehicle. In the case of Stephen Fain, he was driving a hire car, and it took some time to get copies of the relevant insurance cover note from the car hire company. Also, he did not live in the town where he committed the offence, and his driving licence was produced at his local police station, while the car documents were separately produced by the hire company. Mr Fain was fined, and had his licence endorsed with five penalty points. He also had to pay prosecution costs.

Some defendants appear before the court several times

before the case is finally over. George Brown was accused of driving with an alcohol level above the limit. At his first appearance, he pleaded not guilty, so the case was adjourned until the trial date fixed by that court. At the trial, the charges against Mr Brown were proved, since the tests at the police station showed an alcohol level in the breath of 48 micrograms of alcohol per 100 millilitres, the limit being 35 micrograms. As he had claimed that his drinks had been doctored by his friends, his solicitor had arranged for a report from a forensic laboratory. Sentencing was deferred until this report was completed, to see whether there were mitigating circumstances for not disqualifying Mr Brown. At the next date, the solicitor explained that, owing to annual holidays by the staff at the laboratory, the report had not yet been completed, and the sentencing was again deferred. Mr Brown was finally fined and had his licence endorsed. But because the laboratory report indicated that he had consumed an unlikely combination of drinks, and that it therefore seemed reasonable that his claim of doctored drinks was true, he was not disqualified from driving.

Motoring courts

Long lists of motoring offences are sometimes dealt with in motoring courts. Indeed, some courts close to motorways hold regular motorway courts, perhaps once a month, which deal exclusively with motoring offences from that motorway. Most motorists plead guilty by post, producing the necessary documents at their local police stations. The driving licence is forwarded to the court dealing with the offence, accompanied by standard forms either confirming the validity of the other documents or stating that they have not been properly produced. The magistrates decide the sentence, and the clerk arranges for the driver to be notified of the sentence. This is usually a fine plus penalty points on the licence. The clerk has the licences available in court, and if the points already there plus the new ones total 12 or more, the driver will face automatic disqualification under the totting up procedure. As the justices do not usually disqualify in the absence of the defendant, the case will be adjourned so that the driver can appear in court.

The work of the court can be slowed down and made more difficult by other organisations. Simon Dawson appeared before the court charged with driving with excess alcohol, using a motor vehicle with no MOT, no insurance, and not in accordance with the driving licence. Driving with excess alcohol is a very serious offence, which can be punished by imprisonment. Mr Dawson appeared the first time with no solicitor and, on the advice of the duty solicitor, asked for the case to be adjourned so that he could obtain legal representation. When the case was resumed, he stated that he had telephoned a solicitor, who had told him to plead guilty to all the offences. He stated that the reason his insurance and MOT were not valid was that he had only bought the car that day, and had not yet been able to get them sorted out. However, he admitted that he had never held a driving licence, and should not have been driving any car. He also said that he had only had 'a couple of pints' that evening, and the other alcohol must have been 'left over from dinner time', so he thought he was not over the limit for driving.

When asked about his previous record, Mr Dawson admitted that he had been convicted of driving with excess alcohol about three to four years ago. The court clerk asked him to confirm the spelling of his name, then explained that there was no record of this conviction from the driver licensing centre at Swansea, probably because Mr Dawson had never been issued with a licence. However, since the criminal record number was now available, the national police computer should be able to supply details.

Since he pleaded guilty, Mr Dawson expected to be sentenced for the offences. But in view of his previous record of driving with excess alcohol and with no driving licence, the magistrates decided to ask for a pre-sentence report from the probation service. They also hoped that by the time the case was heard again, full details of Mr Dawson's previous record would be available.

Even when a case should be straightforward, complications can occur. Carol and Clive Black, a mother and son, were accused of jointly assaulting Vera Walker. Vera was a former girlfriend of Clive who his mother had never liked. The couple had eventually parted very acrimoniously. Carol and Clive had gone out together one evening. They went into a pub where they saw Vera. Clive tripped Vera up, punched her in the face and kicked her. Several witnesses said that they also saw Carol hitting Vera. When asked, both Carol and Clive consented to a summary trial. But when asked for a plea, Carol replied, 'Not guilty', while Clive admitted the offence. A trial date for Carol was fixed, the magistrates agreed to defer the sentencing for Clive until the result of Carol's trial was known, and both cases were adjourned for four weeks. Both Carol and Clive were granted unconditional bail.

Many people are surprised to read in their local newspapers long lists of people convicted of failing to have a television licence, particularly when most of the people on the list are women. There is a simple reason for this: whoever is in the house at the time the lack of a licence is detected is charged with the offence. This can be unfortunate when a babysitter unknowingly watches an unlicensed television set – after all, who asks to see the licence in a friend's or relation's home before watching a programme? In a case like this, although the viewer is technically guilty of an offence, the likely result will be an absolute discharge, which means that no other punishment will ever be imposed.

Some cases evoke pity in the most case-hardened of magistrates. Eunice Jones was an old age pensioner, 66 years old. She lived an unblemished life until the death of her husband, some two years earlier. At this time, she began to steal things from shops. On her seventh appearance in court, the magistrates were told that she had been stopped leaving the supermarket, and found to have a tin of salmon, a jar of mixed spices and a pair of rubber gloves, total value £4.83, in her shopping bag, in addition to the three items she had paid for. Mrs Jones had £10.27 in her purse at the time she was stopped.

Mrs Jones pleaded guilty to the offence, and told the court that she had only her state pension plus £5 per week income support to live on. Her council flat was cold and damp, causing her to have enormous gas and electricity bills, totalling £20 per week. She stole luxury items from shops because she had no money to pay for such things. Many people would think that the simple answer would be to find Mrs Jones a more suitable home, decreasing her heating bills and releasing the money to buy the occasional treat. Unfortunately, the court is a place to administer justice according to the law, and no matter how sorry the magistrates might feel for the defendant, they cannot allow people to carry on stealing goods from shops. On this occasion, Mrs Jones was eventually sentenced to a short period of probation.

When the defendant pleads not guilty to the charges, the case has to go to trial, and inevitably takes much longer. At the initial hearing, when the defendant states his plea, the case is usually adjourned so that sufficient time for the trial can be allocated in the court listings. Although summary trials are much less formal than those in the Crown Court, certain formalities do have to be complied with, and a date convenient for the defence, prosecution and any other witnesses is agreed. It is often impossible to know exactly what really happened, and the magistrates have to do their best to disentangle two (or more) conflicting stories.

Most, but not all, prosecutions are brought by the Crown Prosecution Service (CPS). Officers of other agencies such as water authorities, Department of Social Security, environmental health departments, the RSPCA or trading standards officers can conduct the prosecution case for relevant matters in the same way as the CPS. Farmers and factory owners are sometimes prosecuted by the National Rivers Authority when fertilisers or industrial wastes pollute rivers. Ron Evans pleaded not guilty to pollution offences after fertiliser was washed into the river by a torrential rain storm soon after it had been applied to his field. The River Authority detected illegal concentrations of fertiliser in the river, and said that Mr Evans should have been aware that rain was likely. Mr Evans claimed that he had complied with all normal safety procedures, and could not be held responsible for the actions of unusually severe weather conditions. Mr Evans was convicted, and fined several thousand pounds.

As well as being the ultimate prosecutor in environmental health or trading standards cases, courts sometimes see the local council as the defendant. These cases are usually brought when the council fails to carry out essential repairs to council houses, and the tenant finally takes court action. In most cases, if the case is proved, the council will be obliged to carry out repairs as a matter of urgency, and is sometimes fined as well.

Some very complicated cases are prosecuted by the

Department for Social Security. The most imaginative of novelists would find it difficult to contrive the plots that some people use to defraud the Social Security system. The use of several names and addresses, numerous children and a vivid imagination sometimes enables a persistent offender to receive thousands of pounds of public money to which he is not entitled. Trying to untangle the threads of these complex webs of deceit can take days, and stipendiary magistrates often hear these long cases.

Special courts

When young people under the age of 18 years are charged, they appear before special youth courts. Though criminal behaviour is not condoned, the atmosphere is rather less formal than that in the adult court. Young people will appear in a youth court to answer charges which, if committed by an adult, would be indictable offences, and would therefore be referred to the Crown Court. Even very young children do, however, have to attend a crown court for trial if the charges are particularly serious. In 1993, two boys only 11 years old were convicted at Preston Crown Court of murdering a toddler.

These cases are, thankfully, rare. Youths are more commonly charged with taking and driving cars, assaults arising from fights, burglary and drugs charges – quite enough for most parents to have to come to terms with.

Every petty sessional division holds regular, previously notified, licensing sessions. The annual licensing meeting will confirm that all existing arrangements continue to be satisfactory, and re-issue the licences if necessary. Other licensing sessions are held when needed by the demands of the area, and may be weekly, monthly or every two months. These make variations to licences, perhaps if a new publican takes over a pub or a new manager is appointed to an off-licence shop. They also grant or refuse applications for occasional extensions to the normal licensing hours, perhaps for a party, wedding reception or other celebration. Some routine licensing work, such as hearing applications for variations to licences, is also heard in the ordinary adult courts.

Before granting a licence, the justices have to be satisfied that the place to be licensed is suitable, and that the person applying for the licence is a fit and proper person to hold a licence. The health and safety or fire department may oppose the application for a licence if the premises do not meet the necessary regulations. Similarly, the police may oppose the licence if there is a serious risk or past history of alcohol-related problems connected with either the premises or the prospective licensee. If a particular pub or restaurant has its licence revoked twice, there must be a delay before anyone can be granted a licence for that place, even if the person making the application had no previous connection with the problem area.

Schools, clubs and other charitable groups sometimes apply for an occasional licence to sell alcohol on a particular special occasion. This is often as a sideline to another function such as a dance, quiz evening or other fund raising event. Again, the justices will ensure that the building is suitable, that the person making the application is a responsible person, and that arrangements have been made to ensure that accurate measures are served. If it is a school, and the event admits children, the applicant will also have to state how the children are to be kept away from the licensed area.

The betting and gaming licensing panel has similar responsibilities for regulating the places where members of the public can gamble. In most towns, these are restricted to betting shops and bingo halls. The justices must be satisfied that both the premises and the person applying for the licence are suitable, and that there is a need for the establishment in that place. Gaming, defined as playing games of chance for money, as opposed to gambling on the result of some event, is severely restricted to a very few private gaming clubs.

Magistrates' courts do not only hear criminal cases. As well as the care proceedings and adoption hearings dealt with in the family courts, magistrates adjudicate in the enforcement of fines, dog orders, abatement of nuisance orders, and people who are bound over.

If neighbours frequently disagree about the condition of a fence or the noise of a record player, tempers can become very frayed. After a period of time, one or the other can lose control, and violence can erupt. Even without violence, one party sometimes gets so fed up with the situation that they ring for the police. If it seems justified, both can find themselves explaining the nature of the dispute to the magistrates. Where the justices are satisfied that this is just a neighbourly dispute allowed to get out of hand, they may order both parties to be bound over to keep the peace. This can only be done with the consent of the people being bound over. The binding-over order should stipulate a sum of money to be paid if the order is broken. But unlike bail conditions or a conditional discharge, breach of the binding over is a civil matter, not a criminal offence.

The enforcement panel is another elected group of magistrates on each bench, who hear cases of failure to pay fines and Council Tax.

As has been seen, there are many different panels and committees that magistrates serve on in the course of their duties. All magistrates take a share of the work of the adult court, the busiest of all the magistrates' courts. The induction training undertaken by newly appointed magistrates centres on the work of the adult court, and this is the only work done in the early years.

After about five years, magistrates are usually invited to undertake chairmanship training, which enables them to chair a particular court session. The court chairman is the spokesman for the justices sitting that day, but his opinion does not carry any more weight than any of his colleagues. He is first among equals. It is possible that three qualified court chairmen may sit one day. Another day, the chairman may sit with two inexperienced colleagues, but they may disagree with him about a particular decision. In these cases, he must give the decision of the majority, with no indication of his dissent.

Magistrates with a particular interest may seek to be elected to one of the panels and committees which hear specialist cases. Individual magistrates may be elected to several of these panels, though as all involve a certain amount of additional work, it is unlikely that anyone would sit on all panels at any given time. These committees are the liquor licensing committee; betting and gaming licensing committee; family panel; youth court panel; and sometimes an enforcement panel. All justices serving on these specialist panels will undertake training in the work of that panel when first appointed, and regularly afterwards. This training will be included in the 12 hours every three years which are required by the Lord Chancellor's Department.

Even out of court, there are many tasks demanded of magistrates. Either before court starts in the morning, or afterwards, they may be asked to sign search warrants and warrants for arrest. These are usually signed in batches at the court, but, exceptionally, police officers may call a magistrate at home and ask for a warrant to be signed.

Although court rotas are decided in advance, criminals

and the police do not take holidays at weekends and bank holidays. Some types of crime, such as gang fights and football violence, are more common at these times than at others. Also, police officers may use these times to arrest suspects they have been looking for. Arrested suspects cannot usually be held for questioning for longer than 24 hours without being charged. A superintendent can authorise the extension of this time to 36 hours but, at the end of this time, a warrant must be obtained from the court, and the suspect is entitled to argue his case before a magistrate.

In other cases, it is desirable that visiting defendants should be returned to their homes as quickly as possible, rather than being detained. In most courts, the clerks have a rota for working on Saturday mornings and bank holiday Mondays. They liaise with police officers, and notify the on call magistrate if necessary. Defendants who plead guilty can often have their cases completed that day. Those who plead not guilty, or do not consent to summary trial, will have a bail application considered, and be either remanded in custody or granted bail and allowed to return home until the date of the next hearing. Summary justice in these cases is not only heard as a result of the issue of a summons – it is quick as well.

Since there are only 52 Saturdays plus bank holidays each year, if most of the experienced magistrates on the bench agree to take a share of the dates, no one will have to give up more than one or two weekends each year.

Appeals

If a defendant or his solicitor disagrees with the decision of the magistrates, an appeal can be made to the High Court or Crown Court. The High Court occasionally hears appeals from magistrates' courts by any of the parties involved, but will only consent to hear the case if it is alleged that an error has been made on a point of law or jurisdiction. For people dissatisfied with the magistrates' decision in a family proceedings case, the appeal is made to the Family Division of the High Court. In all these events, the appeal is made to a judge.

The Crown Court hears appeals against decisions made in criminal cases in magistrates' courts, and also, occasionally, appeals against the refusal to grant a licence application. These appeals are heard by a judge and two magistrates. One of the magistrates will usually be from the same petty sessional division as those who originally heard the case, to provide continuity and local knowledge. This magistrate will not have been present at the original hearing. The other will be from a different petty sessional division.

It is important that magistrates undertake crown court duties, so that there is continuity in the decisions being made. It is particularly important that local justices share the hearing in a licensing appeal, since the reason for refusing the application may not be obvious to someone who does not know the location of the proposed premises. An application for a licence to operate a bingo hall will probably be refused if it is only just around the corner from an existing hall. This may not show by simply giving the address.

If most of the magistrates on the bench offer to share the crown court duties, each will only have to attend a maximum of two or three times a year. Each crown court will call on all the justices from the petty sessional divisions which commit cases for trial at that court.

Once the work in all the courts is completed, some magistrates choose to give time to other related committees. Most benches have committees which liaise with other agencies involved in the administration of justice.

These can include the probation liaison committee, court users' groups, magistrates' courts committee and county probation committee. Others attend meetings of the county branch of the Magistrates' Association.

All these meetings are valuable ways of keeping in touch with other people who are involved with the administration of justice. The probation liaison committee, for example, has representatives from both the magistrates and members of the probation service. Any problems which are being experienced locally, such as long delays in preparing pre-sentence reports or the lack of accommodation in bail hostels, can be discussed in a calm manner, away from the pressures of the court room. Much goodwill is created, and problems are often solved before they become insurmountable.

Magistrates are also used as a community resource. They are occasionally asked to hear, and validate, statutory declarations. But by far the most common request is to endorse passport photographs as a true likeness of the person applying for the passport. Since the form asks the person endorsing the photograph to state whether they have known the person making the endorsement for at least two years, it should be relatively easy for the magistrate to be honest in his dealings with his friends and neighbours in these matters.

Although this outline of the work of a magistrate seems daunting, magistrates are only required to sit for a minimum of 26 half days a year. If a justice sits in the licensing or family court on a particular day, that is instead of, not in addition to, a sitting in the adult court. Each bench estimates the expected volume of work for each specialist panel, and appoints or elects sufficient justices to carry out that work. A justice who seems to be carrying too great a load will be asked to examine his sittings, as will someone who seems to be falling behind.

Although few magistrates claim to enjoy the office – after all, how many people enjoy the thought of sending others to prison or fining them? – most derive great satisfaction from it. The office of Justice of the Peace is an ancient and honourable one. It is the bedrock of British justice, and needs a constant influx of ordinary men and women to maintain the worldwide respect for British justice.

Appendix: Origin of the Magistrates' Court

The ancestry of today's magistrates' courts can be traced back to William the Conqueror and his successors. Then, as now, many crimes were officially committed not against another individual, but against the King's Peace.

Three modern reminders of this system are experienced Barristers being appointed Queen's Counsels, the offence of Disturbing the Peace, and the fact that in most criminal cases the indictment reads 'The Queen v Fred Bloggs' or 'Regina v Fred Bloggs', followed by the legal statement of the charge. People are also sometimes 'bound over to keep the peace'. In early times, the King made the laws, and was expected to hear all cases personally. If he did not or could not, the victim and his family felt entitled to exact retribution in the form of a blood feud. In the absence of a police force and national judicial body, the law was difficult to uphold and justice was inevitably rather crude.

Since there were no road traffic acts, licensing

regulations, television licences, employment laws or divorce, most disputes tended to be about violence, stealing or land disputes. Some offences, such as adultery, came under the auspices of a very powerful Church, and much litigation was about the possession of land. At this time, the King owned all the land in the country, and it was held by various barons and nobles on behalf of the King. In return, the nobles paid taxes to the King, related to the value of the land, and were also liable to provide soldiers and their equipment in times of war or civil unrest.

Life expectancy was short, and many nobles left young children as their natural successors. They often also had younger brothers (and, sometimes, sisters) with an eye to the land while the child heir was young. It was up to the King to decide who was to administer the land on his behalf, and under what conditions.

In those days the widow of a wealthy man, particularly when she had no sons or only very young children, could be arbitrarily married off to almost anyone as part of a land deal. Indeed, she was often seen as of less importance than the land involved. If she refused, the only real alternative was a convent. A hard choice for a young widow to have to make.

In peace time, the King and his *Curia Regis* (Royal Court) travelled around the country, dispensing justice as appropriate, and collecting taxes as they went. In fact, the collection of taxes was the main object, and resolving disputes was incidental, only important because the King wanted to know who was to pay the tax due from a particular tract of land! The method of settling disputes was to select a jury. Unlike a modern jury, which is not allowed to have any prior knowledge of the case, early jurors were chosen because they did have local knowledge of the matter, as well as of the people involved. The

King and the *Curia Regis* held an inquest, at which the jurors who appeared were more like modern witnesses. They stated, from their own knowledge, where boundaries had been in the past, what landmarks had been used to define boundaries, the wishes of the dead person if inheritance was the problem, and the characters of the people involved.

At a time when travel was a slow and dangerous undertaking, the Kings gradually began to stay in London, where the most serious cases or those involving powerful dukes and earls were brought to them. Other cases were decided locally, by officials appointed by the King. In addition, the royal courts began to be more interested in crime. Felons had always been dealt with locally, but in a rather arbitrary fashion. Some areas were harsher than others, and some sheriffs were more zealous in tracking down the criminals. At a time when the lords of the land had absolute control over the lives (and, often, deaths) of the serfs and villeins who came with the land, many harsh sentences were meted out for what we regard as relatively trivial offences. Justice, like many other things, has to be seen in the context of the time.

By the end of the twelfth century, local people had a duty to present suspects, to charge them with their offence first before the sheriff, and then before a royal judge. By this mechanism, all serious crimes were brought to justice. At this time though, communities were much smaller and isolated from each other, and there was no police force, so local people had to use their own knowledge to arrest their suspects.

Until the early thirteenth century, those accused were put to an ordeal. In the ordeal of water, a priest would pray over the water, and forbid it to accept a liar. The accused would swear to his innocence, and be lowered into the water. If he floated, his oath was shown to be false, and he was therefore guilty of the offence. If he drowned, it is presumed he was innocent! However, as the property of convicted felons was forfeited, it was to the benefit of his family to die unconvicted, as they then retained a means of supporting themselves. It was not until the Church decided in 1215 that the whole system was based on superstition and forbade priests to take part that trials by ordeal ceased.

In the sixteenth century, the justices of the peace began to make and record preliminary examinations before presenting the case to higher courts. This continues today, during committal proceedings. The magistrates examine the evidence against the defendant, and have the power to dismiss the case if they consider that there is not enough evidence to justify a full trial. The defendant is cleared of the offence.

Over the next few hundred years, many types of court evolved and were amalgamated to suit the times. In the Middle Ages, divorce was rare, and a separate divorce court an unnecessary indulgence. Today, divorce is more common, and the family courts are kept busy making arrangements for the care of children and the disposition of homes and incomes.

Glossary

Adjourn To postpone, or break off and continue at a later date.

Aggravate To increase the gravity of the circumstances. Aggravating factors can lead to an increased sentence.

Appeal To ask a higher court to formally re-examine the case.

Bail To release a defendant until the date of the next hearing. Bail can be either unconditional, or have specific conditions applied.

Bench The group of magistrates who serve a particular area; the three magistrates sitting in court on any day.

Clerk A legally qualified officer of the court, who makes official notes of the proceedings and advises about legal matters.

Committal The legal process of referring a case for trial in the Crown Court.

Community service order Sentence of the court, where the offender makes reparation by working for a set number of hours for the benefit of the community, without payment.

County Court The place where serious civil matters are heard. These are often financial cases.

Court chairman One of the three magistrates sitting at any given time, who speaks on behalf of his colleagues. He occupies the centre chair, but his views do not have any priority over those of the other magistrates.

CPS Crown Prosecution Service.

Crown Court The place where criminal cases are heard before a judge and jury.

Crown Prosecution Service (CPS) An independent government agency, which employs qualified solicitors and barristers to prepare the prosecution evidence and plead in court in most criminal cases.

Custody Imprisonment.

Defendant The person accused of a crime.

Evidence The facts, testimony or articles which tend to prove a point of view.

Indictment The formal accusation of the offence for indictable offences.

Magistrates' Court The place where criminal and civil cases are heard by magistrates.

Mitigate To decrease the gravity of the circumstances. Mitigating factors can lead to a decreased sentence.

Offence The legal definition of the law which has been broken.

Offender Person who commits an offence.

Order The sentence or decision of the court – for example, probation order, community service order, or licence endorsement.

Petty Sessional Division The area served by a bench of magistrates.

Prima facie From the Latin meaning at first sight. A *prima facie* case is one where there is, at first sight, enough evidence against the defendant to justify a trial. If there is not enough evidence, the magistrates will dismiss the case.

Probation order Sentence of the court involving regular meetings between the convicted person and a probation officer. Aims to reduce the likelihood of re-offending by examining the circumstances surrounding previous offences, and obliging offenders to consider the effects of offences on their victims.

Probation service The independent government services which administer probation and community service orders, and prepare pre-sentence reports when required.

Remand To send back, either in custody or on bail, if the case against the defendant is not completed.

Stipendiary magistrate A legally qualified paid magistrate, who sits alone. Stipendiary magistrates often hear summary offences or committal proceedings where there are a lot of co-defendants or where it is expected that the hearing will run to several days, as few lay magistrates are able to sit for many consecutive days.

Summons The formal accusation of the offence, for summary offences.

Trial The legal process to decide whether the defendant committed the offence when he pleads not guilty.

Warrant Instruction to police to arrest the person named on the warrant. Warrants can be backed for bail, where the person is arrested but given bail to appear before the court, or without bail, when the person will be arrested and held in a police cell until the next sitting of the court.

Wingers The two magistrates who sit with the court chairman.

Witness Someone who appears in court at the request of either the prosecution or defence to say what he saw or heard about the matter.

Index